THE CHICAGO PUBLIC LIBRARY

TRAILBLAZERS OF THE WILD WEST

GOLD MINERS
OF THE WILD WEST

Jeff Savage

ENSLOW PUBLISHERS, INC.

44 Fadem Road   P.O. Box 38

Box 699   Aldershot

Springfield, N.J. 07081   Hants GU12 6BP

U.S.A.   U.K.

Library of Congress Cataloging-in-Publication Data

Savage, Jeff, 1961–
    Gold miners of the Wild West / Jeff Savage.
        p. cm. — (Trailblazers of the Wild West)
    Includes bibliographical references and index.
    ISBN 0-89490-601-1
        1. Gold miners—West (U.S.)—History—19th century—Juvenile literature.
2. West (U.S.)—Gold discoveries—Juvenile literature. [1. Gold mines and mining.
2. West (U.S.)—Gold discoveries.] I. Title. II. Series.
F591.S327 1995
979'.02'0922—dc20   94-41931
                                                                CIP
                                                                 AC

Printed in the United States of America

10 9 8 7 6 5 4 3 2 1

Illustration Credits: The Bancroft Library, University of California, pp. 4,
15, 17, 39; Denver Public Library, Western History Department, pp. 26, 41;
E.A. Hegg, negative no. 97, University of Washington Libraries, Special
Collections Division, p. 34; E.A. Hegg, negative no. 157, University of
Washington Libraries, Special Collections Division, p. 33; E.A. Hegg, nega-
tive no. 412a, University of Washington Libraries, Special Collections
Division, p. 40; E.A. Hegg, negative no. 578, University of Washington
Libraries, Special Collections Division, p. 36; Library of Congress, p. 13;
Montana Historical Society, p. 22; Kristin McCarthy, p. 11; Nevada Histori-
cal Society, p. 20; Samuel A. Osgood, New-York Historical Society, p. 7; *New
York Tribune*, p. 27; J.G. Wilson, Denver Public Library, Western History
Department, p. 29.

Cover Illustration: Paul Daly

❯❯❮ CONTENTS ❮❯❮

James Wilson Marshall (1810–1885) discovered gold at Sutter's Mill, near present-day Sacramento, California.

1

A GOLDEN DISCOVERY

James Marshall strolled about, breathing in the frigid air, inspecting the grounds, as he did every Monday morning. The men on his crew were preparing for another hectic workweek. They were building John A. Sutter's water-driven sawmill.

Only about fourteen thousand United States citizens lived in California at the time. On January 24, 1848, something was about to happen in the sleepy town of Coloma that would change everything.

Marshall examined the newly built tailrace, the small canal that discharged the water leaving the mill. Three days earlier, the workmen had dammed the south fork of the American River in order to direct a flow of water through the mill. Marshall saw that the tailrace was working well.

That was not all he saw. The river had swept away

rock and rubble, leaving silt in part of the tailrace. Marshall glanced up at the dam, then back at the sawmill and tailrace. Looking closely at the silt and noticing something shining in the early morning sun, he wondered if he could be seeing things. He squinted as he looked even closer at the silt. The dirt sparkled.

Marshall scraped up some of the silt in his hand, and rubbed it with his fingers. Shiny flakes and small nuggets separated from the dirt.

For years, Marshall had heard rumors about gold in the foothills of the Sierra Nevada mountain range. Could this be gold? He bent over and gathered up more silt. More small gold nuggets appeared. James Marshall was an excitable man to begin with. On this morning, his heart was pounding. He grabbed a rock, and hammered a nugget with it. The gleaming metal flattened easily as gold should. Fool's gold, which looks like real gold but is worthless, would have broken into bits. Marshall was sure now that he had discovered gold!

For two days, Marshall wondered what to do. Should he tell the workmen? What if they killed him and hoarded all the gold? Should he keep the secret to himself? How would he be able to concentrate on building the sawmill? Finally, he decided to tell his boss, John Sutter.

Marshall rode forty-five miles to Sutter's Fort, arriving there on January 28. He was sweating from excitement as he burst into Sutter's office.

"He told me he had something of the utmost importance to tell me," Sutter wrote in his diary, "that he wanted to speak to me in private, and begged me to take him to some isolated place where no one could possibly overhear us."[1]

Sutter and his bookkeeper were alone in the house. Marshall insisted on going upstairs with his boss, and Sutter obliged. The two men entered a private room. Marshall began to tell of his discovery. He took a piece of cloth from his pocket and began unfolding it. Suddenly, the bookkeeper walked in to ask Sutter a question.

"My God, didn't I tell you to lock the door?" Marshall yelled.[2] Sutter sent the bookkeeper out, then

John A. Sutter (1803–1880), was one of the first American settlers in California, when it was still a province of Mexico. With permission from the Mexican government, he founded a settlement near present-day Sacramento in 1839.

convinced Marshall that the bookkeeper had no idea what was going on. Marshall took no chances. He bolted the door, then pushed a wardrobe against it. Then he removed from the cloth a few of the gold nuggets that he had discovered at the mill. Sutter looked closely at a nugget. "Well, it looks like gold," Sutter said. "Let us test it."[3]

The two men looked in Sutter's encyclopedia for some of the different ways to test gold. They pounded the nuggets. They weighed them in water. They dipped them in nitric acid to see if they resisted corrosion; gold wouldn't come apart in the strong acid. The nuggets passed all the tests. Marshall definitely had found gold.

Marshall returned to Sutter's Mill where he told the workmen about his discovery. At first, they were not excited. They continued to build the mill, and only dug for gold on Sunday—their day off. When the mill was finished, some of the men began to spend all their time prospecting for gold. The news spread to San Francisco, and eventually to the East Coast. Most people did not believe that gold had been discovered. They thought it was a trick to get people to settle in California.

Reports continued to be published. A letter was printed in the November 1848 issue of the *American Journal of Science and Arts*. The last paragraph read: "Gold has been found recently on the Sacramento, near Sutter's Fort. It occurs in small masses in the sands of a new millrace, and is said to promise well."[4] Still, most of the eight hundred people who lived in San Francisco didn't react.

Then one day, a man named Samuel Brannan got people excited. Brannan lived a few miles below Sutter's Fort, and he had opened a supply store for miners. Not many customers came. So, Brannan filled a bottle with gold dust, and rode to San Francisco. He walked up and down the streets, held the bottle of gold dust high over his head, and shouted, "Gold, gold! Gold from the American River!"[5] Before long, fewer than a hundred people were left in San Francisco. The rest were digging for gold near Sutter's Mill. First, of course, they stopped for supplies at Sam Brannan's store.

Easterners began taking this gold talk seriously. Wild tales were being spread, first of nuggets of gold, then boulders of gold, then mountains of solid gold and rivers gleaming with gold. The rush was on!

John Sutter was disappointed that gold was on his property. He owned thousands of acres of land that he named Nueva Helvetia ("Helvetia" is the Latin name for Switzerland, the land of his ancestors), and filled it with horses, cattle, mules, sheep, and hogs. Sutter just wanted to manage his land and watch his herds increase. For him, this gold rush could spoil everything.

⇥◁ 2 ▷⇤

THE CALIFORNIA GOLD RUSH

The gold "discovery" of 1848 probably came as no surprise to some. Native Americans probably knew for centuries about gold in the area, but they had no use for it. Mexican authorities used it in small quantities for jewelry and decorations. Yankee traders from the East would take home tiny nuggets or flakes, mainly as souvenirs. The Native Americans and Mexicans also knew that news of a gold rush would lure thousands of white settlers.

In fact, gold had been mined in California some years earlier. Francisco Lopez, a Mexican cattle rancher, discovered gold northwest of Los Angeles, in the San Fernando Valley, on March 9, 1842. Lopez was returning home that day from tending his cattle in Placerita Canyon. On the way home, he remembered to pick some wild onions for his wife. As he pulled the onions out of the ground, Lopez noticed that shiny particles were

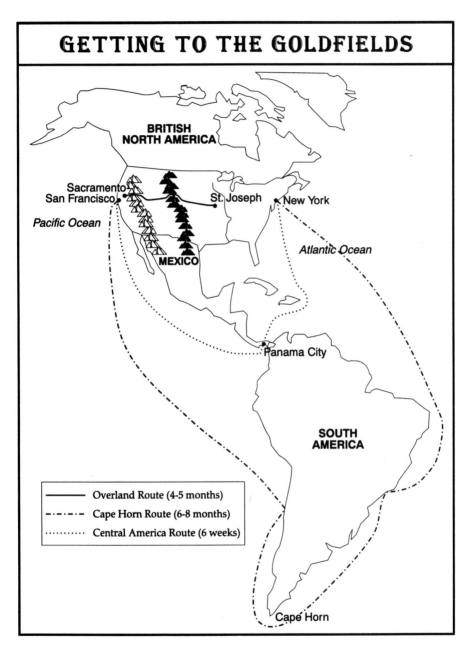

GETTING TO THE GOLDFIELDS

BRITISH NORTH AMERICA

Sacramento
San Francisco

Pacific Ocean

St. Joseph

New York

Atlantic Ocean

MEXICO

Panama City

SOUTH AMERICA

Cape Horn

——— Overland Route (4-5 months)
— · — · — Cape Horn Route (6-8 months)
· · · · · · · · Central America Route (6 weeks)

In 1849, most Americans lived east of the Mississippi River. There were three ways for Forty-Niners to get to the goldfields of California. All three could be dangerous, as well as expensive.

attached to the onion roots. He had found gold! A local gold rush followed, and the land was worked over.

Getting There

Thousands of United States citizens packed their belongings and set out for California in 1848. Emigrants living in New York, Massachusetts, or other states along the East Coast had a choice of routes. Many sailed south on clipper ships to South America, around Cape Horn, and up the Pacific Ocean to San Francisco Bay. It was a long and expensive journey, but not as physically demanding as other routes.

Others traveled south by boat to Panama. There they crossed the Isthmus of Panama on foot. Hiking across the Central American country in the oppressive heat was difficult. Reaching the Pacific Ocean, they sailed north to California.

Emigrants from the Midwest had to take the overland route. The most common route, and certainly the cruelest, was the overland route. There were northerly trails, southerly trails, and rugged paths over the Sierras. It was hot and dusty in the summer, then cold and wet as winter arrived. Along the route, food was difficult to come by. Clean water often was scarce. Wagon trains broke down. Horses died. Emigrants crossing Native American territory were considered intruders, and were attacked. The trails were littered with tragedy.

For safety, travelers were advised to go west across

A miner shows two others how to pan for gold. Miners later realized the real money was in the rocks and mud lining the creeks.

America in groups that included at least four grown men. One popular guidebook author, D. C. Oakes, wrote that six months on the trail required, among other things, twenty-five pounds of gunpowder and fifty pounds of lead (for bullets).

John Goller

John Goller, a prospector from Illinois, traveled to California in 1849 with a group of other miners. Goller's group decided to avoid the colder northerly routes. They would cross Death Valley to the south. It was a bad idea. For fifty-two agonizing days, Goller's party struggled to cross the hot, barren wilderness. They went for days without food or water. One man died, and another went crazy and wandered away.

When the survivors finally made it to civilization, Goller had with him a handful of gold nuggets. He had found them somewhere in Death Valley, but he could not be certain where the mine was. Instead of going north, Goller decided to stay in Los Angeles. He spent the rest of his life leading expeditions in search of the lost mine. He never found it.

All through 1849, as people arrived in the Golden State, they were met by thousands more who poured in from Asia, South America, and Europe. These masses of gold prospectors became known as the Forty-Niners.

The Miners

Miners came from everywhere. Their backgrounds were as varied as the land in which they dug. Before trying their luck at prospecting, they might have been doctors, lawyers, editors, or lawmen. One writer said, "All mixed together you had shrewd New England business-men, rollicking sailors, Australian convicts and cut-throats, Mexican and frontier desperadoes, hardy backwoodsmen, professional gamblers, whiskey-dealers, general swindlers . . . professional miners from all parts of the world."[1]

Chinese immigrants poured into California in the 1850s in search of gold strikes. Although they were eager to find gold in what they called the Gold Mountain, they suffered from race discrimination at the hands of white settlers. The Chinese were prohibited from

Miners work a stream in the foothills of the Sierra Nevadas.

working the best mines, yet they proved industrious by squeezing out the remaining gold from old diggings. In many communities, they worked for very low wages as cooks or laundrymen.

Staking a Claim

Prospectors could not just dig anywhere they wanted. They had to make a claim on an area of land. If no one else had filed a claim on this piece of land, it could be claimed by the prospector. Nobody was permitted to search for gold on another person's claim. Those who did were called claim-jumpers. Sometimes, they were shot by claim owners.

James Marshall, the man who discovered the gold at Sutter's Mill, was forced by a gang of miners to leave his own claim. Even John Sutter, on whose land the gold had been discovered, lost out. His land was grabbed, and he spent a fortune in legal fees trying to reclaim it.

Getting the Gold

Would-be prospectors had much to learn about mining. They couldn't just stroll along gathering gold nuggets. There were several methods used for digging gold.

The simplest method, panning, was used around rivers and creeks. Panning required a tin pan about three or four inches deep and a foot or so wide. Gravel was scooped into the pan, water was added, and the pan was skillfully swirled. Since gold is heavier than dirt, the silt spilled out of the pan, and the gold remained in the pan. This gold on the surface of creek beds was called placer gold.

When the placer gold along rivers and creeks had been removed, miners began to use larger equipment. Cradles and long toms were contraptions that separated the gold from the mud. They were flat wooden troughs, sometimes thirty feet or more in length, that stretched along the river. Mud would be shoveled into the troughs and then would be washed from one end to the other. A screen or a series of ridges were built into the top end of each trough. They would hold the heaviest material—the gold—while the dirt would wash away. Because these tools were costly to build, mining began to get expensive. People formed partnerships to share the cost.

Some miners eager to dig were too poor to buy even the simplest tools. That is where grubstaking came in. A backer would outfit the miners with needed tools, and supply them with food, in return for a share of whatever they found. H.A.W. Tabor was one such grubstaker. Tabor gave seventeen dollars to two prospectors in Leadville. A year later, they presented him with his share of their find—a million dollars. Most grubstakers, like most miners, never got rich.

Mining was not only a grueling business; it was hazardous as well. Miners had to be wary of claim-jumpers and bandits. It was hard to survive in bad weather. As prospecting became more elaborate and mines were built, one out of every three men who worked in a mine for at least a decade suffered a serious injury; one out of eight got killed. An estimated 7,500

Mining camps were lawless wild settlements. Makeshift bars provided one of the few local entertainments.

men died in mines, and another 20,000 were badly wounded.

Mining Camps

There was plenty of gold in California. Nearly $600 million in gold was mined from the ground by 1860. Another $700 million was found between 1860 and 1900. Most of the placer gold, however, was skimmed away within the first year.

By the end of 1850, only one in a hundred panners was making a decent profit at mining. The names of the mining camps reveal their disappointment and despair. Among the camps and diggings were Poverty Flat, Dry Diggings, Bed Bug, Drytown, Mad Mule Gulch, Git-up-and-Git, Loafer Hill, Murderer's Bar, and Rough and Ready.

By 1866, there were more than one thousand mining camps in the West. They varied in size and shape, usually depending on the amount of gold nearby. One observer described them this way: "The typical camp of the gold prime of '49 was flush, reckless, flourishing, and vigorous. Saloons and gambling-houses abounded; buildings and whole streets grew up like mushrooms, almost in a night. Every man carried a buckskin bag of gold-dust, and it was received as currency at a dollar a pinch. Everyone went armed. A stormy life ebbed and flowed through the town."[2]

⇥ 3 ⇤

THE COMSTOCK LODE

The Mother Lode was the name given to the gold deposits in California. The lode ran along the western side of the Sierra Nevadas. It was quickly overrun with miners. On the other side of the Sierras—the eastern side—there were but a few specks of gold on the surface, and fewer prospectors. The terrain east of the mountain range was mostly dry and barren. This was the high desert country of the Utah Territory (later Nevada).

Throughout the 1850s, miners would pause for a few days on the eastern side of the Sierras to search for gold before continuing west to California's Mother Lode. Finding the yellow flakes scarce, they would move along. These miners had no idea that they were standing on a precious metal of another sort—silver! They didn't know what silver ore looked like, so they simply shoveled it aside.

The few prospectors who did live in the high desert managed to scratch out a living. Among them was Henry Comstock, a gruff man who was nicknamed Old Pancake after his favorite food. One of Comstock's friends was James Finney, who was called Old Virginny. While staggering along the road drunk one night, Old Virginny dropped a bottle of whisky. When it smashed on the ground, he looked up and shouted, "I christen this ground Virginia!"[1] The town became known as Virginia City.

Comstock and Finney each had a claim of the legal size, measuring fifty feet wide and four hundred feet long. When the two miners began to find traces of gold

Henry Comstock sold his claim for $11,000. Later, millions of dollars in silver was mined from his property.

in 1859, they named the area Gold Hill. They each made about twenty dollars a day—very good money at that time.

Two Irishmen, Patrick McLaughlin and Peter O'Riley, showed up one day at Gold Hill. Finding the area claimed, McLaughlin and O'Riley hiked a short distance to Six-Mile Canyon, where they began to dig. About four feet down, they struck a layer of blue-black sand. Thinking nothing of it, they dug deeper until they found a pale dust. It was gold, they were sure, but something was wrong with it. The blue-black sand had lightened its color.

Henry Comstock showed up one day at Six-Mile Canyon. He inspected the pale flakes of gold, then claimed the area as his own. He said the Irishmen were on his ranch, which was a lie. Comstock would not allow them to continue digging unless he and a friend, Emanuel Penrod, were given half the profits. McLaughlin and O'Riley reluctantly agreed. For the next month, the four miners tossed aside the blue-black sand to get to the pale flakes of gold. Each day they turned up hundreds of dollars in gold.

Finally one month later, a settler on the Truckee River decided to have the blue-black sand examined. He carried a sack of it west over the Sierras to Grass Valley, California. The settler took the sand to an assayer, a person who examined the minerals to find out how much they were worth. The assayer could not believe

Once the placer gold had been cleaned out of an area, miners would smash apart local stones. They hoped to find veins of gold inside ordinary rocks.

the test results. The blue-black sand was worth $3,000 in silver and $876 in gold per ton.

By the next morning, it seemed that every citizen in Grass Valley had heard about the silver and gold. Hundreds of men raced across the Sierras to the high desert. There, they found the area from Gold Hill to Six-Mile Canyon already claimed.

When Comstock and his partners were told what they had, they celebrated. Comstock roamed up and down the area, bragging so loudly that the entire region of blue-black sand became known as the Comstock Lode.

James Finney was the first to sell his claim to the new arrivals from Grass Valley. Some say all he got in return was a horse, two blankets, and a bottle of whisky. Comstock followed, selling his claim for $11,000. He later invested the money in a supply store, and lost it. A decade later, the poor man wandered to Montana where he shot himself. Comstock's friend Penrod sold his claim for $8,500, then disappeared. McLauglin sold his share for $3,500. He became a cook for other miners, and died penniless. O'Riley was smarter. He held on to his claim until he was offered $45,000, a sum he couldn't refuse. Soon, however, he went insane, and began wandering the countryside carrying a pick and shovel, but never digging.

The newcomers kept their wits about them. They invested in heavy machinery, and dug deep shafts. Thousands of miners from the Mother Lode joined them in the digging. More than $1 million worth of silver and gold was pulled up the first year, and twice that the second. The sum reached $6.24 million in 1862, and doubled again the next year. In 1869, a railroad was built from Virginia City to Nevada's territorial capital, Carson City, to haul supplies and the loot. A massive amount of metal worth $38.57 million was dug up in 1876—and it was immediately dubbed the Big Bonanza.

In the first thirty years, from the time the discoverers sold their claims until 1890, the Comstock Lode yielded nearly $400 million in silver and gold. Just as California is called the Golden State, the state of Nevada officially became the Silver State.

⭐ 4 ⭐

OTHER WESTERN RUSHES

On January 6, 1859, a few months before the rush for silver in Nevada, another discovery was made. As usual, it was more a matter of luck than anything else. A prospector named George Jackson had been roaming with his two dogs through the snowy Rockies in search of gold. Jackson was about thirty miles west of Denver, in what was then Kansas Territory (the Colorado Territory had not been created yet). The young prospector was an experienced miner, having spent several years working California's Mother Lode with the Forty-Niners. When Jackson ran out of food, he decided to quit exploring for gold. On his way back to Denver, he came upon a meadow where the snow had been melted by a hot spring. He decided to search for gold one more day.

Jackson tramped through the snow along the frozen

south fork of Clear Creek. Then he saw it: a gravel bar that sparkled underneath the ice. He built a bonfire on the ice to thaw it. Then he reached in and broke off a chunk of the bar. When he swirled the dirt and rock in his drinking cup, a few tiny gold nuggets were left at the bottom.

He had no mining tools with him. The frozen ground was too hard to dig through anyway. Jackson covered up the signs of his discovery, then marked the place so that he could it find later. He would return to the area after the spring thaw by following his secret treasure map. When he reached Denver, then only a town of some twenty cabins, he wrote in his diary: "After a good supper of meat—I went to bed and dreamed of riches galore in that bar. If I only had a pick and pan instead of a hunting knife and the cup. I could dig out a sack full of the yellow stuff. My mind ran upon it all night long. I dreamed all sorts of things—about a fine house and good clothes, a carriage and horses, travel, what I would take to the folks down in old Missouri and everything you can think of—I had struck it rich! There were millions in it!"[1]

Jackson was partly right. More than $100 million in gold would be lifted from the south fork of Clear Creek, but he did not gain the riches he imagined. In May, he returned with some friends to the area. In six days, they panned out $1,900 worth of gold. Soon after, Jackson sold his portion of the claim for a small sum.

Leadville, Colorado, was founded in 1878 when silver ore was discovered nearby. By 1880, the population of the town was more than 30,000.

Jackson's discovery wasn't the first in the Rocky Mountain area. Tiny flakes of gold had been seen in these parts for a few years. The joint discoveries of the Comstock Lode and Clear Creek seemed to signal the start of a mad dash by more than one hundred thousand prospectors to the Colorado area. Hordes of experienced miners traveled from California, and thousands of novices poured in from the East. The rallying cry was "Pike's Peak or Bust"—named after the landmark mountain nearby.

Horace Greeley

Many Easterners were inspired by the newspaper stories of popular *New York Tribune* journalist Horace

Greeley, who wrote firsthand accounts of the gold. Little did anyone know that Greeley had been tricked.

Greeley arrived in Denver determined to see the gold for himself. The townsfolk welcomed him, and sent him off to a mining camp. Greeley was such a proud man that the miners decided to fool him.

One way to sell a worthless claim is to sprinkle flakes of gold dust in an area where a buyer is likely to pan. When he finds the flakes, he is sure that the claim has gold in it. This is called "salting a claim."

When Greeley arrived at the camp, the miners already had salted an area for him. They showed him how to pan for gold properly. Greeley then proceeded to pan at the salted spot. At the bottom of his pan he found several gold flakes. He panned a second time

Horace Greeley (1811–1872) was the editor of the New York Tribune. *He was well known throughout the United States for his views opposing slavery. He ran for president in 1872, but lost to Ulysses S. Grant.*

with the same sparkling results. "Gentlemen," he announced, "I have examined your property with my own eyes and worked some of it with my own hands and I have no hesitation in saying that your discovery is what it is represented to be—the richest and greatest in America."[2]

When he returned to New York, Greeley wrote about his trip in the same excited way. Then he gave this famous order: "Go west, young man." Plenty of people followed his advice.

Cripple Creek

Bob Womack was working on a ranch at Cripple Creek, Colorado, in 1878, when he found a small chunk of rock that contained gold. It appeared to have drifted down the creek. Womack had the chunk assayed, and found the gold to be worth two hundred dollars a ton. Now it was just a matter of finding the vein from which the chunk had come.

Womack spent the next decade wandering drunk around the area, digging holes for miles around. People laughed at him, and they called him Crazy Bob. His search paid off in 1890, when he struck the vein in Poverty Gulch, not far from where he had found the original chunk of rock. Cripple Creek had been explored by real miners years earlier, but no gold was found. The townspeople weren't about to believe Crazy Bob.

Womack didn't care. He started digging a shaft for

Cripple Creek was one of the great rushes in Colorado.

his mine, and eagerly showed the locals more chunks filled with gold. They refused to give him the money he needed to develop his mine. Instead, two other prospectors made strikes of their own totaling more than $200,000 worth of precious metal. The rush was on. By 1893, more than 10,000 prospectors were digging in the area. By 1900, Cripple Creek's population had swelled to 25,000, and $18 million in gold was found. Womack's mine produced more than $3 million, but Womack didn't get any of it. In a drunken state, Crazy Bob sold his mine for three hundred dollars and left the area. He died broke.

The Dakotas

In the late 1870s, two brothers, Moses and Fred Manuel,

found rich deposits of gold near Deadwood in the Black Hills of the Dakota Territory. The Manuels mined what they could with their simple equipment. Then they sold their claim, which they had called the Homestake. The Manuels were paid $150,000 (a great sum at the time) for their mine, and were instantly wealthy. Others certainly got rich off the mine as well. The Homestake Mine was probably the richest single mine in the world, eventually producing more than $1 billion in gold.

❈ 5 ❈

THE KLONDIKE

———◆•◆•◆———

Gold fever reached its peak in 1897. Several dozen men sailed into Seattle, Washington, and came ashore with mounds of gold. This sight triggered the wildest rush for gold in the history of America. The headlines in the *Seattle Post-Intelligencer* read: "GOLD! GOLD! GOLD! GOLD!—Sixty Eight Rich Men on The Steamer *Portland*—STACKS OF YELLOW METAL!"[1]

One man tried to lift a suitcase so heavy with gold that the handle snapped off. Another gave his unsuspecting wife a sack that held $100,000 worth of gold—an enormous fortune. Another man and his son returned with $112,000 in gold.

Within weeks, everyone had heard of the Klondike. The Klondike is a part of the Yukon Territory in northwest Canada. It seemed as though every prospector in America was on his way there. In 1897, at least two hundred thousand people set out for the Klondike. Most never made it, getting there was a terrific ordeal.

Discovery

No more than a dozen prospectors panned for gold along creek beds in the Yukon Territory in 1870. Twenty years later, there were about 2,500 men looking for gold. In 1895, they managed to find more than $1 million in gold. Still, it wasn't enough to lure the grizzled veteran miners of California, Nevada, and Colorado. Too many of them had journeyed into hills before, only to come up empty-handed.

The frenzy began when an American named George Washington Carmack poured a shotgun shell of gold dust onto a saloon counter for all to see. Carmack and two Native American friends, Tagish Charlie and Skookum Jim, had found a huge deposit of gold along Rabbit Creek. Prospectors from Forty Mile and from the nearby town of Dawson soon were panning along Rabbit Creek, which immediately was renamed Bonanza Creek. At Bonanza Creek, and a few miles south at Eldorado Creek, more than two tons of gold were found in the next few months. Carmack and his two friends would be among those who showed up in the Seattle harbor with hundreds of thousands of dollars in gold.

Getting There

The Klondike gold rush will forever be remembered not

Miners needed to carry loads of supplies with them on their voyage to the Klondike.

for the riches, but for the trip. All the work was in getting there.

There were two main ways to reach the town of Dawson from the south. One was to sail by steamer around the Aleutian Islands to Alaska's west coast, then 1,355 miles up the Yukon River. This could be difficult, because the Yukon is frozen much of the year. Once a boat reaches an icy portion of the river, it is locked in until the next spring's thaw. The other way to reach the town was to cross some of the most treacherous land on the continent. From the Skagway or Dyea ports in Alaska, miners crossed the Alaskan coastal range. They had to choose between White Pass, with its steep cliffs and ghastly swamps, or Chilkoot Pass, with its harrowing climb.

Prospectors hauled a ton of food and supplies with them. If they didn't, they would run out before the end of the six-month trip to Dawson. The last four miles over the Chilkoot were so steep that climbing them took almost all day. The job of hauling a ton of baggage over the pass, carrying no more than eighty pounds a day, sometimes took three months to finish. The route got so

Masses of eager miners climbed the treacherous Chilkoot Pass.

treacherous at times that men climbed on their hands and knees. Often, horses were used to climb White Pass, but there were so many hazards that thousands of the animals died along the trail.

Once over either the Chilkoot Pass or the White Pass, the miners had to cross a string of lakes and rivers. This was a frustrating task as well. One man hauled a ton of food and supplies over the Chilkoot to Lake Lindemann, where he built a boat. Rushing down the rapids, the boat crashed into a rock and everything was lost. The man trudged back to the starting point, bought a new load of equipment, and spent another three months hauling it over the Chilkoot. He built another boat, and again lost everything in the rapids. The man swam ashore, grabbed a gun, and killed himself.

Living in the North

Not everyone suffered such tragedy. By mid-1898, there were 28,000 people in Dawson. A few were women and children, but most were men hoping to strike it rich. They were known as Sourdoughs, because every prospector kept a bowl of sourdough bread starter in his cabin.

When winter arrived, the cold was devastating. The temperature sometimes dropped to 75 degrees below zero, while 38 below was considered mild. In the summer, it might warm up to 100 degrees or above. Just below the ground there was a permafrost that never thawed, even in summer. It made digging in the Klondike all the more difficult. Each night, miners would build bonfires at the bottoms of their shafts, melting away perhaps six inches by morning. It sometimes took all summer to get deep enough to reach gold.

When a prospector hit pay dirt, he knew it. The ground was so rich with the precious metal that a single shovelful could yield $800. Some prospectors did indeed get rich. Fred Bruceth panned $61,000 in one day. Big Alex McDonald, who was known as "The King of the Klondike," once found a single gold nugget that weighed nearly four pounds. Lucky Swede Anderson was tricked into paying $800 for a supposedly worthless

The winter months are brutal in the Klondike region. Miners often had to wait until the spring before their shovels could make a dent in the frozen ground.

claim, then got the last laugh when he dug out $1 million in gold from it.

As quickly as it started, however, the Klondike gold rush ended. There was little ground left to dig, and far too many diggers. The gold was gone. Prospectors began leaving, first in a trickle, then in a rush. The Chilkoot and White Passes were nearly as clogged with people going as they had been with people coming.

Only one fourth of the estimated two hundred thousand people who set out for Dawson made it there. Of those, only half looked for gold. Of the four thousand who found gold, maybe four hundred got rich.

⚛ 6 ⚛

THE END OF THE RUSH FOR GOLD

In the goldfields across the land, simple panning and wooden troughs eventually became obsolete. Big businesses with giant machinery moved in, replacing the crude methods of mining. With their chance of getting rich on their own now slim, prospectors began working for large companies that sifted through tons of dirt and rock each day.

Mining Becomes Big Business

Gold and silver deposits were known to be deep in the earth, but getting there required intensive labor. Enormous caves were dug using hand drills and sledges. Compressed-air drills were great for drilling holes into granite or quartz, but they stirred up clouds of razor-sharp particles that lodged in men's lungs and caused silicosis, an often fatal disease.

Miners journeyed deep underground to dig up ore from which gold and silver were removed. Stamping machines crushed the ore into a fine paste. The ore was then placed in large steam-heated pans, and the precious metals were chemically extracted.

Mining Dangers

Black gunpowder was often used to blast through rock. This powder was packed into a hole generally the depth of a finger and ignited by a fuse. In the 1870s, dynamite

This drawing of the mining operations on the Comstock shows the lengths to which miners would go to find gold.

As miners dug deep into the earth, the dangers became more serious. Cave-ins, explosions, and choking dust caused numerous deaths among men and boys.

replaced black powder. Dynamite was about four times as powerful as gunpowder, but it was also more dangerous. Explosions sometimes caused cave-ins or released deadly fumes. When dynamite was introduced to mining, many more miners died than before.

One story in an 1891 Colorado newspaper told of four men who were "torn and mangled beyond recognition" after an explosion in a Clear Creek mine.[1] Mining explosions were so common that most never even made the news. One occurred in 1900 at the Winter Quarters Mine in Scofield, Utah. More than three hundred men were in the No. 1 and No. 4 shafts when a low thud was heard. Black powder had exploded, filling the shafts with a deadly gas. In moments, more than two hundred men were killed. Death came so quickly that some of the dead miners were found still holding their tools.

Why did prospectors risk their lives in such dangerous exploits? Most did it in the hope of someday striking it rich, not because they wanted to live as rich men, but for the thrill of finding wealth.

Settling the West

The mining boom did something else as well. It led to the settlement of the West.

Before the gold rush in 1849, the California non-Native American population was about fourteen thousand. A dozen years later, it had ballooned to 380,000. Gold was discovered in Columbia, California, in March

Known as the "Miner's Angel," Nellie Cashman was a successful miner who donated much of her wealth to help others.

1850. A month later, the town had grown from 300 to 8,000 people. By the end of that same year, Columbia had 30 saloons, 143 gambling houses, 53 stores, 4 hotels, and 4 banks. Virginia City, where Old Virginny had dropped a bottle of whisky and named the town, exploded in the early 1860s into a metropolis of 20,000 people, which included 3 undertakers, 4 churches, 100 saloons, and about 19,000 starry-eyed miners.

For every prospector who struck it rich, there were a hundred or more who died poor. Most of the time, mining was a thankless, luckless, punishing business. Each miner, no matter what his fate was, had a story to tell, the same story of being close to fabulous wealth, having the riches within reach, and trying to improve his lot in life. It was the story of miners.

In 1954, prospector James Williams stumbled across a lost mine in the hills around Salmon City, Idaho. The mining tunnel he found was so old that in the middle of its entrance was a tree more than fifty years old. Inside, Williams found its walls so rich in gold that he could pick out nuggets with his fingertips. Why was the gold still there? What had happened to the owner of the mine? He may have been killed by a bear, a bandit, or another miner. Or he simply may have lost his way back to the mine.

⇥◉ NOTES BY CHAPTER ◈⇤

Chapter 1
1. Ralph K. Andrist, *The California Gold Rush* (London: Prentice-Hall International, 1961), p. 18.
2. Ibid.
3. Ibid., p. 19.
4. Gordon V. Axon, *The California Gold Rush* (New York: Mason/Charter, 1976), p. 13.
5. Ibid., p. 29.

Chapter 2
1. Vardis Fisher, *Gold Rushes and Mining Camps of the Early American West* (Caldwell, Ida.: The Caxton Printers, Ltd., 1968), p. 98.
2. Ibid.

Chapter 3
1. Robert Wallace, *The Miners* (New York: Time-Life Books, 1976), p. 60.

Chapter 4
1. Robert Wallace, *The Miners* (New York: Time-Life Books, 1976), p. 19.
2. Vardis Fisher, *Gold Rushes and Mining Camps of the Early American West* (Caldwell, Ida.: The Caxton Printers, 1968), p. 69.

Chapter 5
1. Robert Wallace, *The Miners* (New York: Time-Life Books, 1976), p. 206.

Chapter 6
1. Robert Wallace, *The Miners* (New York: Time-Life Books, 1976), p. 103.

➤◀ GLOSSARY ▷◀

assayer—A person who tests mineral ores to see if they contain any valuable metals.

backer—A person who provides the money for mining a claim. A miner would do the actual panning and would share the gold with the backer.

claim—A piece of land that a miner has made his own. All the rights to the minerals in that claim are his. A typical claim was about 50 feet by 400 feet.

cradle—A long wooden trough used by miners to separate gold flakes and nuggets from mud and silt from the bottom of a creek bed. They would fill the trough with mud and water, and then they would rock it until the mud separated from the heavier minerals, like gold.

desperado—An outlaw.

fool's gold—A mineral that looks like gold, but is worthless. Pure gold is soft and malleable, and can be beaten into sheets. Fool's gold is hard and breaks apart if it is struck with a hammer. Its scientific name is pyrite.

grubstaking—Working a claim using money supplied by a backer. The miner does all the mining work, and the backer provides the money and tools needed to mine, getting a share of the gold that is found.

lode—A mineral deposit.

long tom—A mining device resembling many cradles attached to one another. Mud was thrown into the trough, and water was poured down. The mud would wash away, and the heavier gold would remain.

panning—Using a shallow, wide pan to search for gold. Scooping up water and mud from a creek bed, the miner would swish the water to separate the sand and dirt from larger rocks that might have been gold.

placer gold—Gold that is found at the surface of creek beds and can be panned easily.

salting—A practice used to sell a worthless claim. The seller sprinkled a few flecks of gold around the claim. When the buyer inspected the claim, he saw the planted flecks, and may have thought the claim was valuable.

silt—The sediments deposited on the bottom of a creek or riverbed.

stake—Another name for a claim.

tailrace—A trough where minerals are separated from silt.

⤐◉ FURTHER READING ◐⤙

Chambers, Catherine E. *California Gold Rush: Search for Treasure.* Mahwah, N.J.: Troll Associates, 1984.

Franck, Irene M. *Manufacturers and Miners.* New York: Facts on File, 1989.

Roberts, Margaret. *Pioneer California: Tales of Explorers, Indians, and Settlers.* San Francisco: Bear Flag Books, 1982.

Stein, R. Conrad. *The Story of the Gold at Sutter's Mill.* Chicago: Children's Press, 1981.

Waldorf, John Taylor. *A Kid on the Comstock.* Reno, N.V.: University of Nevada Press, 1991.

Wallace, Robert. *The Miners.* Alexandria, Va.: Time-Life Books, 1976.

✦ INDEX ✦

47